CH

Michelle Obama

CHERRY LAKE PRESS

Published in the United States of America by Cherry Lake Publishing
Ann Arbor, Michigan
www.cherrylakepublishing.com

Reading Adviser: Marla Conn, MS, Ed., Literacy specialist, Read-Ability, Inc.
Book Designer: Jennifer Wahi
Illustrator: Jeff Bane

Photo Credits: ©cate_89/Shutterstock, 5; ©Obama White House/flickr, 7, 9, 11, 13, 15, 22; ©DFID - UK Department for International Development/flickr, 17; ©Faizal Ramli/Shutterstock, 19, 23; ©Elaine Sanchez/Department of Defense/Public Domain, 21; Jeff Bane, cover, 1, 6, 14, 18

The appearance of U.S. Department of Defense (DoD) visual information does not imply or constitute DoD endorsement.

Library of Congress Cataloging-in-Publication Data

Names: Sarantou, Katlin, author. | Bane, Jeff, 1957- illustrator.
Title: Michelle Obama / Katlin Sarantou, Jeff Bane.
Description: Ann Arbor, Michigan : Cherry Lake Publishing, [2020] | Series:
   My itty-bitty bio | Includes index. | Audience: Grades K-1 | Summary:
   "The My Itty-Bitty Bio series are biographies for the earliest readers.
   This book examines the life of Michelle Obama in a simple,
   age-appropriate way that will help children develop word recognition and
   reading skills. Includes a table of contents, author biography,
   timeline, glossary, index, and other informative backmatter"-- Provided
   by publisher.
Identifiers: LCCN 2019034629 (print) | LCCN 2019034630 (ebook) | ISBN
   9781534158740 (hardcover) | ISBN 9781534161047 (paperback) | ISBN
   9781534159891 (pdf) | ISBN 9781534162198 (ebook)
Subjects: LCSH: Obama, Michelle, 1964---Juvenile literature. | Presidents'
   spouses--United States--Biography--Juvenile literature. | African
   American women lawyers--Illinois--Chicago--Biography--Juvenile
   literature. | Lawyers--Illinois--Chicago--Biography--Juvenile
   literature.
Classification: LCC E909.O24 S27 2020 (print) | LCC E909.O24 (ebook) |
   DDC 973.932092 [B]--dc23
LC record available at https://lccn.loc.gov/2019034629
LC ebook record available at https://lccn.loc.gov/2019034630

Printed in the United States of America
Corporate Graphics

About the author: Katlin Sarantou grew up in the cornfields of Ohio. She enjoys reading and dreaming of faraway places.

About the illustrator: Jeff Bane and his two business partners own a studio along the American River in Folsom, California, home of the 1849 Gold Rush. When Jeff's not sketching or illustrating for clients, he's either swimming or kayaking in the river to relax.

My name is Michelle Obama.
I was born in Chicago, Illinois.
It was 1964. This was the middle
of the **civil rights movement**.

I studied at Princeton University in New Jersey. I went to Harvard Law School in Massachusetts.

I worked at a **law firm**. I met Barack Obama there. We fell in love. We got married.

I also worked at a **nonprofit**.
I worked with communities.

My husband became president. This was in 2009. He was the first African American U.S. president.

I became **First Lady**. I was the first African American First Lady.

I wanted to make the world
better. My focus was on
nutrition. I wanted kids to be
active and healthy.

How can you make the world better?

I supported girls in school.
I helped start the Girls
Opportunity Alliance. I also
supported women and families.

How do you support others?

I wrote a book about my life.

I travel to give talks. I work with the Obama **Foundation**.

I am a role model for women and girls.

I want to **inspire** women of color to find their voice.

What would you like to ask me?

2009

1960

↑
Born
1964

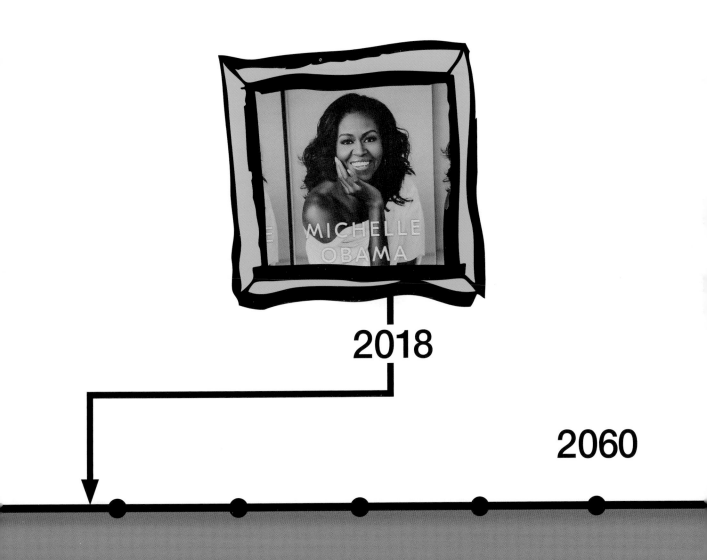

2018

2060

glossary

active (AK-tiv) a lifestyle that involves regular exercise

civil rights movement (SIV-uhl RITES MOOV-muhnt) an effort to fight for the right of African Americans to be treated equally under the law

First Lady (FURST LAY-dee) the wife of the president of the United States

foundation (foun-DAY-shuhn) an organization that gives money to help others

inspire (in-SPIRE) to fill someone with a feeling or idea

law firm (LAW FURM) a place where people trained in the practice of law

nonprofit (nahn-PRAH-fit) an organization whose goal is to aid a worthy cause and not to make money

nutrition (noo-TRISH-uhn) eating and drinking the proper amounts to be healthy

index